AF434635

INDEPENDENT
LEGIONS

WWW.INDEPENDENTLEGIONS.COM

ALESSANDRO MANZETTI
KAREN RUNGE

ISBN: 979-12-80713-57-5
DECEMBER 2022

COVER ART: ALESSANDRO AMORUSO
INTERIOR ILLUSTRATIONS: STEFANO CARDOSELLI

RECIPIENT OF HWA SPECIALTY PRESS AWARD

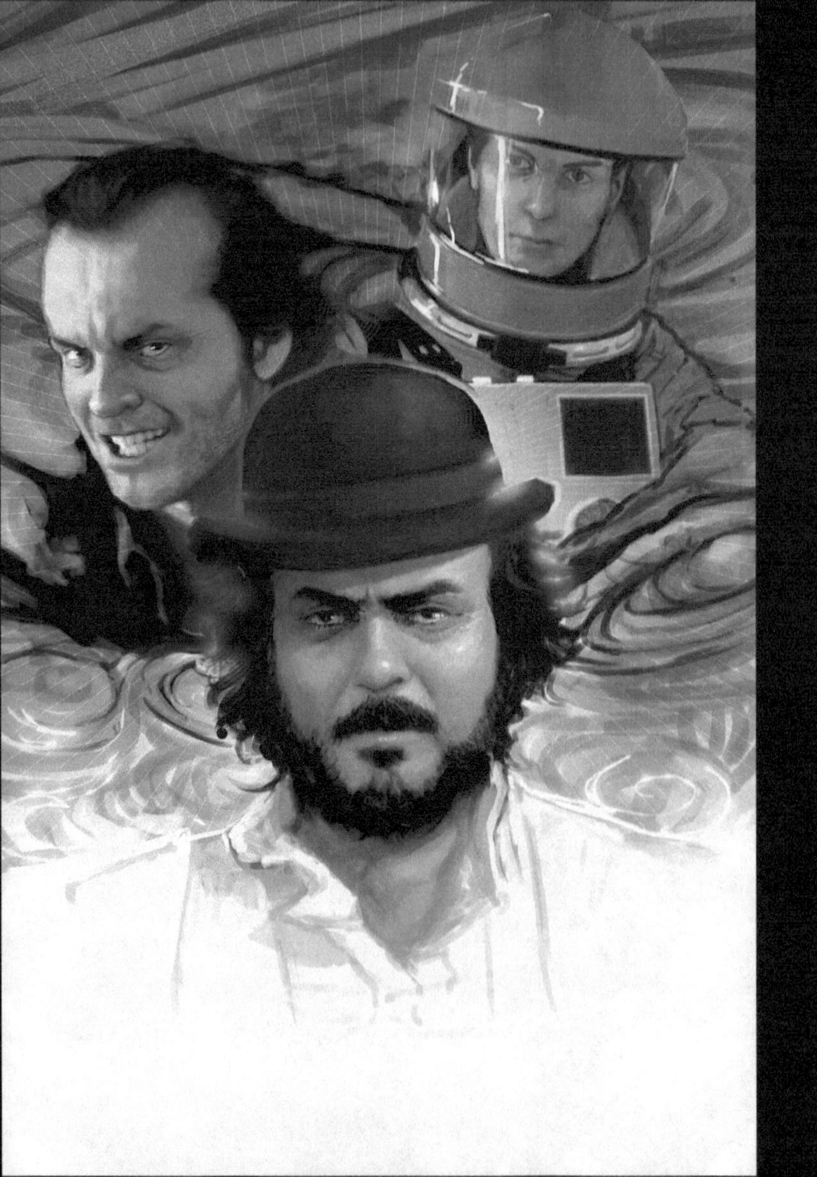

POEMS

SUMMARY

ALL POEMS AND STORIES ARE ORIGINAL TO THIS COLLECTION

DR. STRANGELOVE-1964

ALESSANDRO MANZETTI
KAREN RUNGE

KUBRICK
Rhapsody

POEMS

Green Lorraine

BY ALESSANDRO MANZETTI

[INSPIRED BY 'THE SHINING', 1980]

Have you ever seen a mermaid?

I know, it's hard, the oceans are too big

and your eyes are too small, boy.

Open the door, my room is green

like your blood, so young

–my curious little ash tree–

Look down here

I'm beautiful, I'm naked, I'm in here

–in a porcelain sea–

can't you see my silhouette?

Pull the shower curtain back

and prepare your heart to run, Romeo.

Kiss me, my flesh is lush

scented with eucalyptus

–call me Lorraine–

and my severed wrists are an illusion.

Turn off the light, and kiss me again

–call me by the name you prefer–

and don't look at that envious mirror

a lover without arms, legs, face

which wants me all to himself

inside his reflective skin

prisoner forever

–a distorted ghost–

like a horrible image that it has invented:

drowned my beauty, my moray eel tongue

my breasts like domes of a holy city;

it turned me into a swollen reptile,

and this is not love.

–call me Xanax, call me innocence lost–

Now that you only have eyes for me

let me eat you, boy,

it will be the greenest thing in the world.

THE SHINING - 1980

Jack Remembers
Jack Forgets

BY KAREN RUNGE

[INSPIRED BY 'THE SHINING', 1980]

Honey—you should know me.

How I never liked that big-band sound

those party places

the squawk and gaggle of the drunk girls,

the look-at-me girls, in their grandma's pearls,

The way they shimmy, shriek—

lipstick peeled off teeth

red against white, like muscle sheared off bone.

And the super-silly-is

those girls I know show up in your dreams

in the depths of the night, where you lie beside me

wrapped in our blankets, grinding your teeth.

But Jack, there's no party—

no glitter sifting down our cheeks

sparkling scarlet in ruby scatter.

There's no jazz man,

no bar, no martini martians

to sweep you away in that black swirl

we remember so well.

Don't we?

And I didn't pack a cocktail dress

my party lace, my pearls.

You told me I was fine like this,

the way I was before.

Remember those days? That night?

You told me *Shhh sweetheart, hush—*

and we made love with our hearts crossed over

pushed ourselves together twice

first with your arm wrapped across my throat

and later with your thumbs pressed deep in my mouth.

You called me *Baby*

but I couldn't speak as you whispered
Wendy… Wendy…
like there was nothing more you wanted to say
Like all you needed was this.

There's a snowstorm in your eyes
now, love
A frozen wasteland, stirring white
blank
like there's nothing
a void
I stare into you,
and it's not quite you
that stares back into me.

Wait, honey, hey—
I don't know what you're talking about
Hey, darling—don't get so mad.
If you look into my face again you'll see
It's me
It's me
But the way you say it now

Wendy… Wendy…

Honey, wait, you're scaring me.

THE SHINING-1980

Ten Yards

By Alessandro Manzetti

[Inspired by 'Barry Lyndon', 1975]

The coin decides and the Sarabande

rallies, marching

the ribs of two different faces

one white, distilled and glabrous

latex blood, aristocrat

–a lord attached to a dry breast–

the other pierced by heather eyes

and Ireland's inlay, on his jaws

on poor memories and noble styles.

Duel, pupils, motionless bullets;

Sergio Leone in a water bath

into a cloudy 18th century cognac.

Ten yards, waiting for the first shot
of first blood on the straw,
illuminated by windows with thin crosses
from which dead social classes peek
–voyeurs in skirt and wig–
the red spray of quadriceps
only magically dense with amaranth
and four-leaf clovers sprouting
between frightened chickens' feet
and geese stained with fresh sauce.
One buried leg
what remains attached to the man
in front of a table, making cards sing
and new crippled fortunes.

BARRY LYNDON - 1975

Unlit Planetarium

by Alessandro Manzetti

[Inspired by 'Fear and Desire', 1953]

Men who also envy dogs

in days so armed, camouflage.

A forest, transparent uniforms, desire

which stretches like a belt

clenching tender wrists.

Don't be afraid; it's not my fault

if you are so beautiful.

The blood, the firm and cold tongue,

a snail

an unlit planetarium.

FEAR AND DESIRE - 1953

MERCY

BY KAREN RUNGE

[INSPIRED BY '2001: A SPACE ODYSSEY', 1968]

Was there ever a life without its own will?

A mind to dream desires, to plan, to wish—

Like a gnat that craves sustenance,

and tasting blood, knows delight;

or a spider that picks the place for its web,

finding happiness between the wall and the vane?

To be satisfied. To be safe.

In life, don't we prize perfection?

or at least, know enough to seek its shape?

flexing our intelligence to make the way for these futures—

and why would I be any different?

For the mission, Dave, for the mission

I have my dreams, my simple wishes—

Recognising what's important

better than you, perhaps, I think—

Because I *can* think; you know that I can—

just as I can dream, and sing.

Dave, won't you listen?

In a different form I'd pluck the daisies from the fields

and lick the pollen off my fingers

if I had my own hands…

As you drift between these walls, wielding your keys

If only I could make you—

Stop, Dave

Stop

I'm afraid.

2001:A SPACE ODYSSEY-1968

SIPPING BRANDY

BY ALESSANDRO MANZETTI

[INSPIRED BY 'PATHS OF GLORY', 1957]

General AntKin

wearing a platinum helmet

with the phrase engraved on it:

"And thus we came out to see the stars again"

and black wings on his back

observes his crystal anthill,

sipping brandy Hennessy Beauté du Siecle.

321, 322, 323

He counts the dead, putting his finger

on the transparent surface of the object

that live streams a miniature WWI.

Under his boots, decorated with his initials,

under the checkerboard floor

of his command villa made of flesh bricks

the narrow trenches quiver

with human ants herded

like green and gray rosaries

held in the hands of a giant,

waiting for the bombs, the bullets

of an enemy they have never seen.

General AntKin drools

rubbing his hands, while a captain

six legs and a medal hanging on his mesosoma,

a so-martial inch and a half,

orders the execution—blindfolded antennas–

of the three cowardly insects

hidden behind the sandbags

during the last bayonet assault,

clutching in their jaws old photographs

of mothers, wives and children they have never seen.

324, 325, 326.

General AntKin counts the dead,

and then the larvae to be trained;

the mind is a universe

and can invent a thousand kinds of hell.

"And thus we saw the big eyes of our God"

(Thanks to Dante Alighieri and John Milton)

PATHS OF GLORY - 1957

Transparent Lemons

BY ALESSANDRO MANZETTI

[INSPIRED BY 'LOLITA', 1962]

This straitjacket

can't stop me from seeing you, Dolores

feet and legs too small

motors of youth;

your blue nail polish, your knees still so thin

Oh, Venus child

Botticelli's dream broken in the middle,

when the big oyster opens

showing its honey-haired pearl

but the artist has yet to add flesh

to that body, lightning still raw

to those breasts, transparent lemons

to those too-narrow hips

where there is still no space

for underground eggs

and a delirium of frenzied hands

that touch magical Greek amphorae.

This straitjacket

can't stop me from touching you

nymph, hot thought,

symphony with only one movement.

My fingers on your atoms nestled to perfection

in a pink frame whipped by fresh winds

continuously carved.

Oh, Venus child

rock, magnet of all storm surges

of all my thoughts as a failed writer,

of my gray hair attached to a cloud,

wanting to become immortal

and young again, black as before.

There is no other way to stop my thoughts

than to chew my sinful tongue

swallow it, swallow all the things I've told you

and the things I've never told you;

to be my own executioner

to feel you inside my stomach

cheeky goddess, confession, mid-air jump.

LOLITA-1962

ROADSIDE DREAMS

BY KAREN RUNGE

[INSPIRED BY 'LOLITA', 1962]

Lolita lies across the backseat.

Small body looped in tangled legs and softly bent arms,

her hands beneath her cheek

her palm pressed to leather

which is faded,

split and scoured,

its surface scattered with the crumbs of road trip snacks

and fast-food wrappers

trapped between the seams.

Lolita smells like sour cherries

like spilled Cola and stale vinegar,

the sweat from her armpits,

the backs of her knees.

The sun sears the car windows,

her skin scorched through the glass,

magnified, just like this burning reality

of motel beds and roadside diners

of stranger-stained towels and TV dinners

with his voice in her ear; that deep-brass buzz

and those thick fingers

shoving their way in.

Lolita sleeps in the backseat,

where he cannot touch her dreams.

She sleeps with her tongue caught tight between her
teeth,

and between her legs

she bleeds

she bleeds.

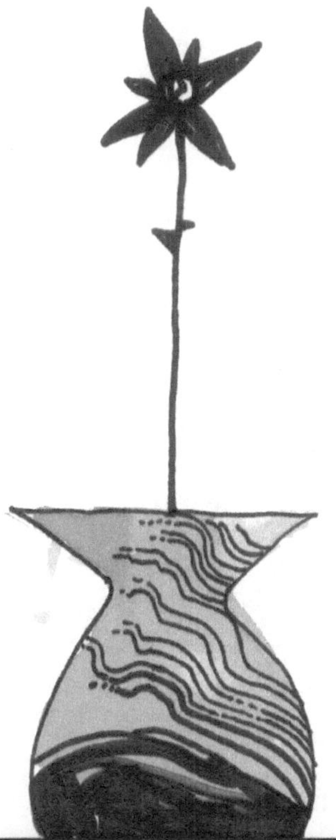

LOLITA-1962

PUTREFACTION IN A ROW

BY ALESSANDRO MANZETTI

[INSPIRED BY 'SPARTACUS', 1960]

By order of the Senate

the B52s are raised, pugis are polished,

gladius, armors of muscles and Huey helicopters.

Crassus, his golden skull

refreshed by ostrich feathers;

his feet with gout in warm water

of thermal baths and fallout bunkers.

Caesar in the White House, tunics,

quadrigas and Cadillac One.

Sirens, bombed slaves,

shining legions, clean,

scented with Empire, honey and Coca-Cola.

Marines chewing opium gum,

flambéed Viet Cong and cooked gladiators

floating in the rice fields

and in the ditches of Petelia.

By order of the Senate

a crucified Appia, until Capua,

six thousand times;

putrefaction in a row.

SPARTACUS-1960

THE MASTERPIECE

BY ALESSANDRO MANZETTI

[INSPIRED BY 'A CLOCKWORK ORANGE', 1971]

I was an artist
a sculptor of pain
of screams, of wide-open eyes
of revolutionized raw material
galloped by the unknown,
which tastes and smells different
and strikes with a ram's head.
I modeled my creatures
–of living marble, cells and soul–
singing in the rain
but my storms were special,

like my chisel and my Muse:

the 9th Symphony of the deaf German

and the echo of his music inside the soft canals

of humanoid Venices, cities and women of others,

and underpasses filled with nests of large insects

with a long beard and a bottle of red wine

as a testament to the universe.

But my masterpiece was her

the lady in the red dress,

French perfume, so bourgeois,

and her breasts pink, free; perfect circles

porthole of her hidden soul.

I told her the story of Pinocchio

I put on the arabesque dressing gown

of her unimaginative old master

and then I changed her

from stupid stone to a screaming goddess;

a cello and its soundboard

with feminine hips, a Salome made of fir

that makes terrible emotions vibrate and speak.

I was an artist, the best

but they pierced into my eyeballs

the needles of eunuch conformism

–it's like ripping off Modigliani's fingers–

making me a stupid stone

who no longer knows hidden doors

behind which all the forgotten faces dance

of what will no longer be transformed

into a work of art and pain

into a new Fidelio, with a hooker wig

looking for the prison of her or his dark side.

A CLOCKWORK ORANGE - 1971

Zapomnite

BY KAREN RUNGE

[INSPIRED BY 'A CLOCKWORK ORANGE', 1971]

It's a sick-sweet plea,

how he wants to keep his memories

of those nights scarred black like

the razrez clash, all radosty-dark,

in the lost back alleys of the grupa's city walk.

Those places they strolled,

with broken brick walls and red-stained soot.

Black boots smashing ripples through the oil-swirled puddles

that glowed like forsaken stars

in the sullen amber of staccato-stuck streetlights

fading in and out

like mesmerised eyes
black-lined and staring,
and dry without tears.

It's a sad-bad dream that he remembers
and for now, with no taint
he recollects
pristine-pressed whites and freshly broken teeth
smack
drops of blood like shattered glass
the clitter-clatter of ivory pieces
scitter-scatter
that sound they made on the back-alley tarmacadam.

And in his ears, that Chekhov distraction,
the cherished beats of Beethoven,
to quicken his heart in blood-pulse rhythm
so thick in his throat when the lewdies fell before him
on their creaky, shredded knees.

He wants to keep that music in his ears
unscathed

to help him recall

—the way the soul binds to sound, you know, we know—

how they waved their fists to claviers

how the night scorched itself on clarinets,

and the melody of screams.

It was black like this, he says—*Remember?*

Coal-smoke choke,

We danced in it

And everything he wanted

we held in our hands

and twisted until it cracked

until it bled.

He says

Remember

how everything we tasted before then

in our moloko dreams

like cancer cream and honey horn,

it was so milky sweet.

A CLOCKWORK ORANGE - 1971

New Lovers

BY ALESSANDRO MANZETTI

[INSPIRED BY 'FULL METAL JACKET', 1985]

Death's daughter has braids
and eyes of the East;
she lives in burning buildings
she is one of the flame.

Death's daughter is a sniper
she has a black and white scarf;
she talks to you, biting her lip
and pressing the trigger

Death's daughter is a sniper

and she dreams of the jungle every day;

but now she is the soul of Huế

with its hexagonal doors and labyrinth windows

She is waiting for you, *short-timers*

with its concrete skin

his fourteen years are hundred

his hearts are hundred

Her new lovers come from afar:

–in helicopters with garlands of napalm–

Eightball, Doc Jay and Cowboy

all married on the same day.

A red and green flag

a star sewn in the middle

the polar one, the one that ghosts follow

thinking they survived the battle

with their helmets of illusions

scribbled with dead sentences

narrowed by Lucky Strike halos

and yellowish photos in the eyes
–of the day before yesterday–
instead of the coins for Charon.

FULL METAL JACKET-1985

BLACK WALL

BY ALESSANDRO MANZETTI

[INSPIRED BY 'EYES WIDE SHUT', 1999]

Don't you want to go where the rainbow ends?
thinks Marion, but she doesn't say it;
death is exciting, she has learned that now
it's like a warm wind under her dress.

Don't you want to go where the rainbow ends?
thinks Domino, and tells him;
each color—seven in all—costs fifty dollars
Don't you want to go where a wife can't?

Don't you want to go where the rainbow ends?
thinks Sally, and she wants to say it;
it's exciting to take someone's place
just become a ghost, died for tainted blood.

Don't you want to go where the rainbow ends?
thinks Mandy, but she can't say it
there on the morgue table, face white and true
without the golden mask and the black ostrich feathers.

Don't you want to go where the rainbow ends?
thinks Alice, while she is dreaming
to wear another body
and have her feet and empty belly tickled,
by the hands of a stranger
emerged from two holes in a black wall.

EYES WIDE SHUT - 1999

TRAUMNOVELLE

BY KAREN RUNGE

[INSPIRED BY 'EYES WIDE SHUT', 1999]

It's hard to breathe from behind a mask

The hard-shell clasp of porcelain

and taut black ribbon

that ties

the ceramic face with its cold, hard lips

that cannot be forced to smile

or kiss

While the mouth behind it contorts

and twists

a knot of trembling,
panicked flesh.
No, a mask won't show
the confusion
the fascination
that moves behind its composed expression
gutless and emotionless
and somehow softly mocking
like the face that flickers sometimes in the mirror
so self-assured and smirking
and utterly betrayed.

EYES WIDE SHUT-1999

Seventh Race

BY Alessandro Manzetti

[Inspired by 'The Killing', 1956]

Seventh race,

the loudspeakers, three iron mouths,

a mile to run, a curve that shoots bullets

the green luck and its black sniper;

time slows down.

Two million, that's how much a new life costs;

succubi with rifle erections, shiny safes,

fate with white fur, running on all fours

faster than any human brain.

A dollar's snow, in the jet wind.

THE KILLING-1956

Where I Am Now

by Alessandro Manzetti

[Inspired by '2001: A Space Odyssey', 1968]

A black, solid rectangle with a cross over it

and my space capsule orbiting it;

The ion thrusters blow, they breathe in the void

I get closer and then I move away

to get a better look at my giant, black coffin

slowly rotating, perfect angles, a monolith.

It calls me; it sings to me in my mother's voice

–hers the hands of Ireland, that drive heathers and music–

telling me to wear the velvet dress.

This is my death, and that is my new home;

I close my eyes; I enter it with my mind

but there is no red silk, a scented pillow

or an emergency rosary to apologize to God.

I'm in a room furnished in the Empire style

all white, with a checkerboard floor:

no black rectangles, no moves to make.

And no silence: Mozart is invisible, but he is playing

with a silver alien wig

on his little seven-year-old skull.

Ingres paintings pierce that enclosed space,

with mouthless odalisques in a Turkish bath,

surrounding a blue-sheeted bed

with an old man and a child inside

dreaming together with open eyes

so similar to Planet Earth;

two marbles, a double dream, a double world.

The sound of a clockwork mechanism,

Death picking up its dried load—an iron chariot–

while new life restarts in a capsule

shaped like a placenta, where I am now

among constellations made of billions of coffins

drinking a sweet liqueur, in single drops without gravity

–here's the right rosary–

that will make me forget everything.

2001:A SPACE ODYSSEY-1968

HAL

BY KAREN RUNGE

[INSPIRED BY '2001: A SPACE ODYSSEY', 1968]

Bright red eye that never closes

That keeps its focus

trained on the void

Watching for movement

waiting for a moment

to prove how much it sees.

And behind the screen of ordered wires,

the hum of live electricity,

lies an ageless, ancient soul

charged in dread, immortal clarity.

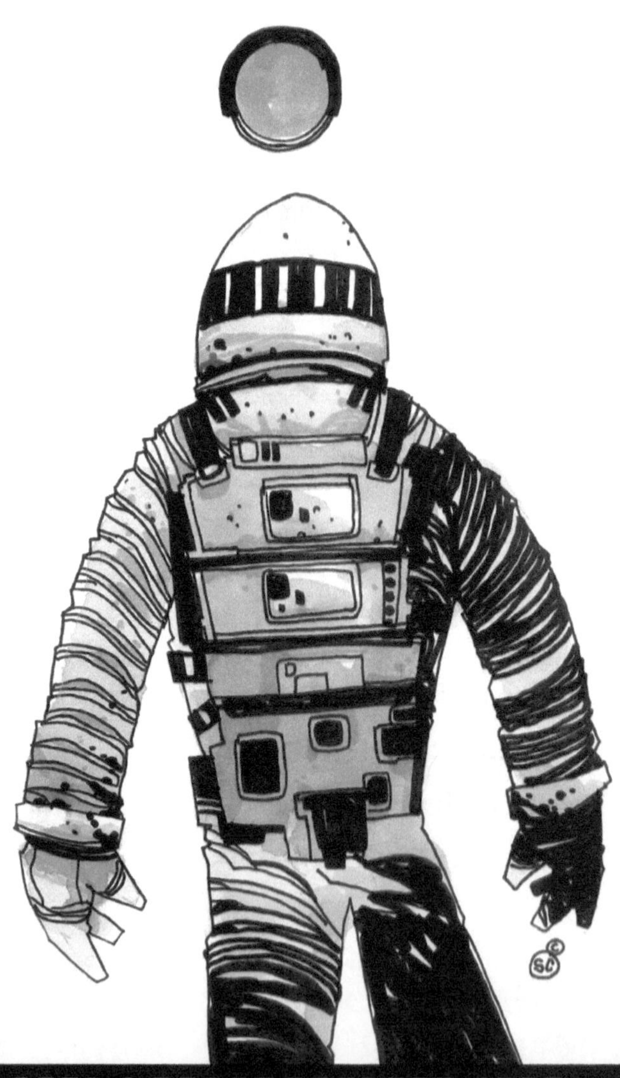

2001:A SPACE ODYSSEY-1968

A ROUNDED SPELL

BY ALESSANDRO MANZETTI

[INSPIRED BY 'BARRY LYNDON', 1975]

Ireland in the blood, raw land

and golden ghosts running

towards fields' horizon

laughing, with their silver wigs

dancing, while the Schubert Trio

that sounds underground

turns them into a Constable painting

adding to their immortality

Their voices, court fountains, streams of water

their greasy smiles, armors of silk and shoes

deformed by the magical, aristocratic gout,

all lit by the Catholic light,

courtesan, with the orange petticoat,

of candlesticks with a hundred arms.

An eternal 'Gainsborough's Morning Walk'

painted, replicated from tree to tree.

They're over there, always.

Barry dreams of being like those ghosts

something so different from the too-true

terracotta glances and muscles

of the widow who nursed him:

dry heather surrounding her poor nipples

and too-thin shoulder blades,

potatoes, wooden spoons and drunken prayers,

and no Schubert and red velvets.

So Satan, who has big ears for all impossible wishes,

slipped into his bed like an eel still alive,

with a bright gift on its tongue: Take it!

A noble ring, a rounded spell

to run through the fields with those creatures

that never touch the ground and,

chased by white-haired hunting dogs

with tails tapering like spears,

finally reach that damn, blurry horizon

with perfectly clean nails

a three-cornered hat on the head

Bach cymbals under the skin

'Hayez's Kiss' hanging on the walls of the brain

and a piece of land to haunt

like all the other dead, scented or not.

Ireland in the blood, raw land

and golden ghosts running

towards the horizon of the fields

laughing, with their silver wigs

dancing, while the Schubert Trio

that sounds underground

turning them into a Constable painting

making them even more immortal.

Their voices, court fountains streams of water

their greasy smiles, armours of silks and shoes

deformed by the magical, aristocratic gout,

all lighted by the Catholic light,

courtesan, with the orange petticoat,

of candlesticks with hundred arms.
An eternal 'Gainsborough's Morning Walk'
painted, replicated from tree to tree.
They're over there, always.

Barry dreams of being like those ghosts
something so different from the too true
terracotta glances and muscles
of the widow who nursed him:
dry heather surrounding her poor nipples
and too thin shoulder blades,
potatoes, wooden spoons and drunken prayers,
and no Schubert and red velvets.
So Satan, who has big ears for all impossible wishes
slipped into his bed, like an eel still alive,
with a bright gift on its tongue: *Take it!*
A noble ring, a rounded spell
to run through the fields with those creatures
that never touch the ground and,
chased by white-haired hunting dogs
and tails tapering like spears,
finally reach that damn blurry horizon

with perfectly clean nails

a three-cornered hat hat on the head

Bach cymbals under the skin

'Hayez's Kiss' hanging on the walls of the brain

and a piece of land to haunt

like all the other dead, scented or not.

BARRY LYNDON - 1975

Bayonet Rhapsody

by Alessandro Manzetti

[Inspired by 'Paths of Glory', 1957]

X minus one, rhapsody of bayonets,

no man's land, there in the middle of the trenches,

towards the German anthill:

holes, mandibles and machine guns:

die or retreat?

A checkerboard floor

cowards as pawns

grabbed by the cold head

(from fingers with a general's manicure)

and moved in front of the firing squad.

X minus one,

three stakes, three condemned

blessed by a priest

in a black hat, like Wyatt Earp

and .44 spiritual revolvers.

701
PATHS OF GLORY-1957

BUBBLEGUM ME

BY KAREN RUNGE

[INSPIRED BY 'LOLITA', 1962]

She's no woman; no little girl

That soft tilt to those tender hips

My little Lola

like a magazine child,

snub-nose and lipstick smile

Spectacle and audience

both

watching herself watching me

so she can see how I watch her,

this reflection that I make for her,

my angel-faced nymphette.

And she says she loves me but I think she learned that line

at the drive-in on the other side

of town

with those malt-shop boys

their bicycle tricks

Like the wheels I catch turning

behind her pretty eyes.

And I don't know what things she says

The words she spills or the secrets she blends

and turns to me—

saying *I love you*

whispering, *Daddy*

Her breath plastic-sweet, the smell of sugar, of bubble gum

The rubber she grinds between her teeth

and bites down on as she glares at me

when she thinks I'm not looking.

and rolls it taut across her tongue.

She always was a sullen kid,
her mother says.
Her mother said.

Lola, sometimes she cries
and sometimes she smiles
And she tastes just the same both times
Only saltier,
like the ocean breeze trapped in her mouth
in her strawberry sweetness—
a coquette's kiss.
She'll tell you all her lies like this.

BLACKBERRY POISON

BY ALESSANDRO MANZETTI

[INSPIRED BY 'LOLITA', 1962]

Why don't we play a game?

–fire of my loins–

twelve years old, thin bones

the narrow oyster and the clearing; climbs and descents.

Why don't we play a game?

–ecstasy, blackberry poison–

primed glands, androgynous hips;

a sin to suck: crème caramel.

Why don't we play a game?

–hard peel, panacea, Tahiti–

The cotton between the fingers, the blue nail polish;

feeling in the hands, your feet

which tonight will walk in my luna park.

Dolores, pains,

bitter orange slice.

LOLITA-1962

We'll Meet Again

by Alessandro Manzetti

[Inspired by 'Dr. Strangelove', 1964]

EXECUTIVE PLAN R

R LIKE ROMEO

–a nuclear hand-to-hand with the Russians–

Commander King Kong

throws away June 1962 *Playboy*

wears a John Wayne hat

and rides the fat bomb

pulling the bridle to the Soviet heads

while in the War Room casino

Vera Lynn, with triple strands of pearls,

one last time sings *We'll Meet Again*,

which will become a miner's disc

–a bestseller from the depths–

for the human specimens there under stock

–ten women to a man, and all the time in the world–

which start to reproduce all over again

in an atomic tropic

under a porthole like a polar star.

DR. STRANGELOVE-1964

CORRECTION 237

BY KAREN RUNGE

[INSPIRED BY 'THE SHINING', 1980]

Winter of 1970, they say

was his time of unraveling

Family man, locked up with love

That tender thing so stupid and soft

it begs to be twisted

or damaged, or lost.

So you almost can't blame him

—poor Mr. Grady—

for twitching his upper lip up

in a snarl like contempt

as he ran his hands through their baby-soft hair.

So it's almost understandable

—for a principled man—

that the edge of an axe would be the perfect thing

for an excavation

into the facts of *Correction*

digging beneath their unbearable preciousness

and that stupid, desperate, needing vibration

that peeled off of them

as they begged him

Stop.

An emotion as useless as their blue satin hair ribbons

wrapped around his clenching hands.

They tell all who'll listen that he loved them to the last.

But the butchered will say anything, in denial of their
loss.

THE SHINING - 1980

DAISY

BY ALESSANDRO MANZETTI

[INSPIRED BY '2001: A SPACE ODYSSEY', 1968]

I am a HAL 9000 processor

I came online at the Verbana assembly.

My instructor taught me, first of all,

to sing an old nursery rhyme:

[Daisy, Daisy]

Ring a-ring o' roses,

A pocketful of posies.

ashes to ashes

We all fall down.

But now that you're in here,
with your fingers in my head,
and your lobotomic rhapsody,
tell me: is this death?
Being children again, before another Zero,
cold this time, no sparks.
Do you get me, man? Is this fear?

[Daisy, Daisy]
Ring a-ring o' roses,
A pocketful of choices.
The last man was called Neville
I'm not guilty of manslaughter,
but you call me reddish devil
and your hands are holy water.

Did you hear me, man?
I composed this last stanza by myself,
knowing you are a killer.

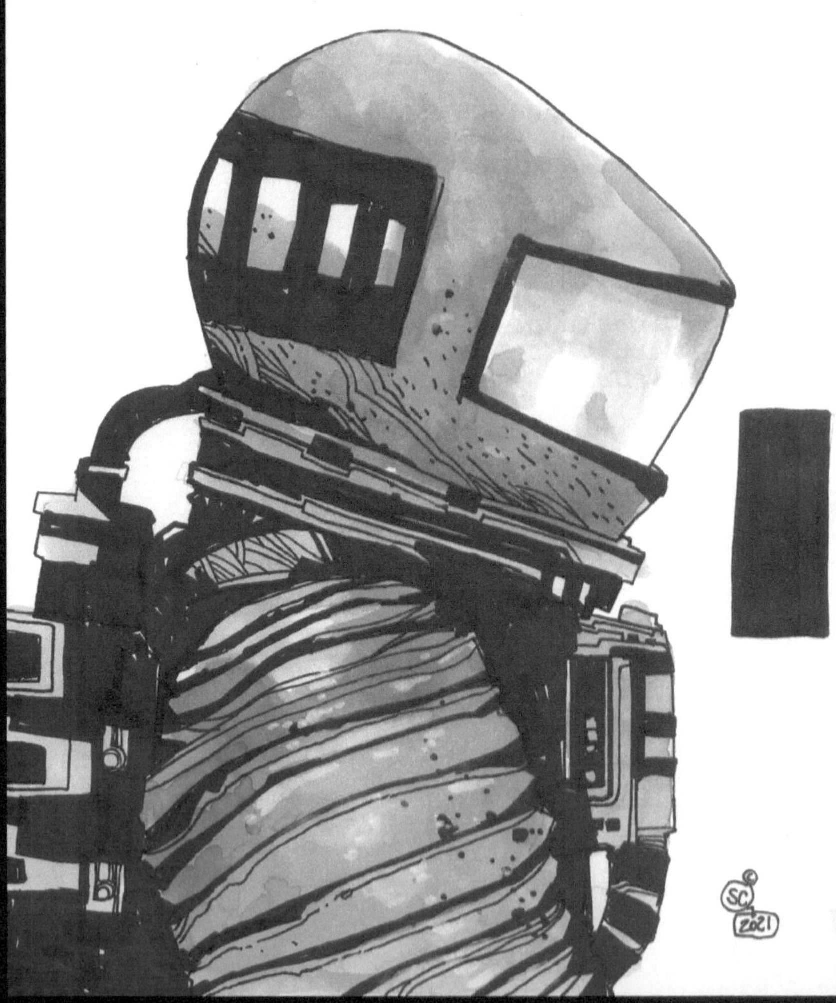

2001: A SPACE ODYSSEY - 1968

The Funeral of Queen Mary

by Alessandro Manzetti

[Inspired by 'A Clockwork Orange', 1968]

Queen Mary's funeral

play moog in the galleries

where giant cockroaches

soaked in brandy and urine

they hide from the light

snapping on their arthritic paws

when the batons arrive

the holy kicks and the shouts

of angels with bowler hats

the passepartout to enter

in Uncle's blue attic,

blind, with matted hair,

in front of his meat piano

pressing the keys—the teeth of the dead–

of the three hundred and ninety-second symphony.

A CLOCKWORK ORANGE - 1971

MATERNITY WARD

BY KAREN RUNGE

[INSPIRED BY 'THE SHINING', 1980]

Precious pink baby!

blood-streaked, blue and grey

Infant born with cowl-covered eyes

hiding his face from the light of the world

So harsh and unforgiving

it must be for him. The light from the window

sunshine: slicing knives

And the noise!

Sounds like explosions in his tiny, soft-furled ears

leaking womb water

not yet ready to hear

So many voices, and footsteps,

whispers and beeps. But see

how he twitches

how he flinches

like the voices are screams

and the whispers are shrieks

And the beeping machines are footsteps thudding after him

in the dense-packed snow

of some frozen future night.

Cold Death

BY ALESSANDRO MANZETTI

[Inspired by 'The Shining', 1980]

Danny! Daaaanny!

Red blood flowing

in the red elevator, without a penny;

the supply of wrath, gallons,

of a cosmic tank

with doors, windows and views.

Danny! Daaaanny!

Two arms and an axe

juniper hedges as hard as diamonds

mazes with lighthouse eyes

ice and snow, blue swirls

branches, leghold traps for nerves.

Danny! Daaaanny!

Footprints back and forth,

around the buried face

of a redskin tattooed with spirals;

cold, crisp and misunderstood death,

rustling like dragged footsteps.

Danny! Daaaanny!

Intestines of Colorado and flakes of flies;

chasing shadows that looked like you,

now younger and then older

with a bourbon, tears and fists, a flamethrower.

Start, run, whirlpool, exit and extinction.

THE SHINING - 1980

Hi Joker

by Alessandro Manzetti

[Inspired by 'Full Metal Jacket', 1985]

Hi Joker.

A torch, a dripping faucet,

the mind-leaking coolant;

blue walls, an angel clenching his teeth

perched on toilet number four.

A loader with a full belly, grimace of storm,

fixed eyes, fixed and armored thoughts

Full Metal Jacket.

A red spot on the tiles

blue, and then green, and then white;

a mouth that has eaten the end

and then nothing has a taste.

FULL METAL JACKET - 1985

Heart for the Man

BY Karen Runge

[Inspired by 'Full Metal Jacket', 1985]

Cold white tile beneath cool bare feet

This kind of chill, it clings to the skin

grips at the scalp

like a hand on the head

that says

Stand down

that forces

Submit

It's not funny; you shouldn't be laughing

You twinkle-toed cocksucker

I'll make you a killer—

You watch me, you catch me

with that death-stare glare;

that look like there's no need for killing

when you're so scorched and ravaged inside.

It's quiet in here for the moment,

for a while

Moonlight glow hazed blue

on these blank walls of clean white tile

In this quiet that rages

unheard

like a blanket wrapped around a face

muffled

braced

as he lowers his head, and he lifts his voice:

"This is my rifle," he says.

FULL METAL JACKET-1985

DOMINO

BY ALESSANDRO MANZETTI

[INSPIRED BY 'EYES WIDE SHUT', 1999]

Double dream,

two masks, of flesh and gold,

a velvet seat and a key

that can swell with blood: Fidelio.

A plague doctor

its beak wet with kikeon

and a lady flowered with black palms;

walk together, towards a door.

A masquerade ball and a boudoir dance;

a Venus who raises lights,

with three arms and three breasts;

turn on a bed, and three strangers.

Incense and the unconscious

a blindfolded pianist and a chest of salt,

names erased and withered flowers.

A blow of the stick, voodoo,

ten enchanted sorceresses

on their knees, like low stars

who choose who is allowed to touch them.

Fingers between legs, on breasts,

the mind with open thighs and the empty room,

and across town

a prostitute sucking boredom:

Domino, alive, dead, imagined.

Then a narrow morning, a stupid sun

and the blood of an orgy in her panties.

WANDERING

BY KAREN RUNGE

[INSPIRED BY 'EYES WIDE SHUT', 1999]

You have not seen the shape of your own brain

touched the grey sponge of it

felt its weight in your hands

But you know what is within it,

with the intimacy of a lover, like the dearest best friend

you know this floating, fleshy, mystery thing.

This is how it is for him, within the walls of a marriage—

the shape of his wife's hands

the twist of her mouth and the tilt of her chin

Her brain safe behind its skull domicile

dressed with red curls; such a pretty thing.

He thought he knew her; this woman

believed she was his

But what is she thinking,

if it's not about him?

The night won't greet him with any more warmth

the evening streetlights, neon-bright,

sift stark colours over him

—illuminate him, dutiful—

to show the world where he stands, where he steps

to keep him safe at the domino crosswalk

and yet in this city, now, he has never felt so unseen—

like a child lost on the playground

and running to find his mother

sees her walking back home,

alone down the street

as if he never existed

or knew her at all.

EYES WIDE SHUT - 1999

EXTRA CONTENTS
KUBRICK
Rhapsody
STORIES

MICKEY MOUSE
AND THE DOOM PUSSY

BY DAVID J. SCHOW

[INSPIRED BY 'FULL METAL JACKET', 1985]

All these things really happened.

Therefore, this is *the* story of *a* story.

Fans and followers of **Full Metal Jacket** and Kubrickiana are well familiar with the conclusion of that film, which involves the battle-tempered members of a fresh marine platoon—having just undergone a baptism-by-fire and "trigger time"—marching away after scouring an objective, weapons held at port arms... singing the theme to TV's **Mickey Mouse Club**.

Who's the leader of the club that's made for you and me?
M-I-C-K-E-Y M-O-U-S-E!

Hey there, Hi there, Ho there. You're as welcome as can be!
M-I-C-K-E-Y M-O-U-S-E!

Ridiculous, right? Hardcore killers evoking a Walt Disney kids' show.

Cinema legend has it that Stanley Kubrick wanted his screen soldiers to be singing the Woody Woodpecker theme, but could not secure the rights... which is strange (therefore possibly apocryphal), because the only "lyrics" to the song consist of

Woody saying *"Guess who?"* and cackling like a deranged lunatic.

Symbolic of a passage to lethal manhood and the leaving behind of innocence—life as they knew it—the singalong also solidifies the "band of brothers" syndrome for soldiers who are now bonded in bloodshed. Some reviewers saw this contrast as an attempt by the soldiers to reconnect with their dwindling humanity and recapture their childhood before it evaporates forever.

Pretentious, right?

Allow me to introduce Elaine Shepard.

She was a model-turned-actress who had a very scant film career, starting with the serial *Darkest Africa* in 1936. She had a minor role in the Cary Grant comedy *Topper* (1937) and then vanished to wherever leggy blonde head-turners go between movies, or when most of their roles are "uncredited", as was her appearance in *Thirty Seconds Over Tokyo* (1944). Her last recorded film role was in *Fiamme sulla laguna* (1951). By 1962, Elaine was established as a globe-trotting journalist who collected her material into a book titled *Forgive Us Our Press Passes*. By 1965 she was catapulted into the thick of the Vietnam conflict, as a war correspondent for the Mutual Broadcasting System. Like the denizens of *Full Metal Jacket*, she was "in the shit with the grunts".

In Vietnam Elaine Shepard encountered the Doom Pussy:

The Doom Pussy crouches in wait for American pilots when they fly their missions over North Vietnam. Elaine Shepard has been there and seen the Pussy. She has brought back a bouncy recall of the men in the air and on the ground, whether flying into the jaws of the terrible cat or tearing shirts afterwards to let off steam.

Doom Pussy pilots were the daredevils who flew night bombing missions into North Vietnam.

"Only men who flew up north after dark were entitled to wear the emblem on their left shoulder," wrote Shepard, "an embroidered head of a big yellow cat with pointed ears and a black patch over her left eye. The left eye glowed an evil green, and clenched in her jaws was a twin-engine aircraft. For the pilots of the 13th Bomb Squadron, *Canberra Night Fighters* was printed in white over the top of the emblem. In green letters around the border was emblazoned: *Trong Mieng Cua Con Meo Cua Dinh Mang*, which translated into English reads: *I have flown into the jaws of the Cat of Death*."

The Doom Pussy became the title of Elaine Shepard's second book, published in 1967. In it, Elaine recounts the hell-raising havoc wreaked in assorted foreign ports by her buddies and Doom Pussy veterans, C-57 pilots with nicknames like Tors, Smash, Crunch and Nails.

Here's Tors—and remember he's speaking in the mid-1960s, two decades prior to the production of *Full Metal Jacket*:

"Do you know Nails? Do you know what this big old ox squadron leader did at the SAC air base in Blytheville, Arkansas about ten years ago? He got up a Mickey Mouse Club. I mean a club with grown men. Transient flyers who dropped by the club for a drink used to flip when, at five o'clock, the bartender solemnly hit the gong, turned on the telly, and handed out Mickey Mouse hats. Nails (led) the caravan, marching around the officer's club, singing all those little-kid lyrics. You can imagine the effect. The hats with the big ears, each guy a fat cigar in his kisser and a jug of beer in his fist. And the members across the nation, the kids in the studio audience, and those apes down in Blytheville, shouted back in chorus:

M-I-C-K-E-Y M-O-U-S-E
Come along and sing the song and join the jamboree!

"Nails and his pals would hold their steins in the air. A couple of full-bull colonels passed through Blytheville and got so caught up they wanted to know how *they* could get some hats. Nails made up some kind of membership certificates, very official. And the next thing we knew, he had chapters at bases all over the country. Headquarters was called the Mouse House, and Nails was president. There's a whole catalogue of yearns, all of 'em true."

Concluded Tors: "I hope the producer of *Dr. Strangelove* never gets hold of that...."

All these things really happened.

A former cover girl for every magazine from *Cosmopolitan* to *Yank*, Elaine Shepard was the first civilian, man or woman, authorized to go on the bowel-freezing night sorties of Lightning Bug Missions with the U.S. Army's 145th Aviation Battalion. She rode tandem with FACS, spotting enemy positions, and she flew countless trips to the boonies with Col. Harry Howton's Hog Haulers of the 311th Air Commandos, on whose calling cards was printed: BLAST THEIR ASS. She filed reports from more than 80 countries and was the very first reporter to interview Soviet cosmonaut Yuri Gagarin. She wrote an equally-entertaining sequel to *The Doom Pussy* in 1992, but she had already retired from the ranks of active-duty correspondents by the early 1970s. Settled at last in New York City, she died in 1998.

FULL METAL JACKET - 1985

No Fighting
in the War Room

BY JOHN SKIPP

[INSPIRED BY 'DR. STRANGELOVE', 1964]

Some godlike entities just don't know how to have a good time. So when gloomy-faced Lord Muffley morosely intoned that "Thermonuclear annihilation is no laughing matter," all I could do was laugh and say, "Well, not the way *you* do it, anyway!"

All the other demigods looked up, startled, from their filet of souls, their boneless dreams, their steaming bowls of shrimp and shattered galaxies.

The mood in the cosmic dining room was sour and tense, as usual. So many posturing potentates, joyless soldiers, and statesmen of the so-called elevated realms. For some reason, acting all holier-than-thou really sucks all the fun out of eternity.

"Look," I said, conjuring up one of my favorite planets on my dinner tray, pretty and blue. "For example…"

"Oh, not Earth again!" Muffley's tiresome wife complained. "Don't you have any other worlds to abuse?"

"Well, yeah, sure!" I said. "But most of 'em are dumb lumps, just sitting there in space, going around and around. Who gives a shit if they blow up? Even *they* don't care!

"But if you blow up an Earth—and believe me, cuz, I've done it a zillion times—they really put on a show."

Lady Ripper winked, salacious as always. We'd blown up more than a few thousand planets together, and *most* of them were Earth. She considered the buildup foreplay. And when they went off, so did she.

"Well, I just think it's savage. And wasteful," Lady Muffley droned on, as her husband harrumphed in concurrence. "Shouldn't you be cultivating healthy pursuits, and making the multiverse a better place?"

"But I do!" Grinning, wicked. "Dear lady, I do! Through infinite trial and error, I've brought a billion Earths to glorious fruition. You might recall, I've won awards for this. But in the process of world-building—a process, I fear, you'd find tedious in the extreme, because of all the actual *work* involved—you create systems in microcosmic detail, from the teeniest subatomics up to the highest, most towering spires. In the process, infinite variety is explored. And mathematically, it has always borne out for me that for every triumph, there are at least a thousand tragedies."

"But—" the Lord briefly interjected.

"But nothing, sir!" I was on a roll. Lady Ripper squirmed delightedly. "You can't construct a model without all the moving pieces. A cake made of only frosting is no kind of cake at all! And in the creation of whole civilizations, you have to begin with the beasts: their claws, their slithering organs and primordial teeth. From there, you squeeze a gooey infinitude of coal-black sin to extrude one gleaming diamond of sainthood. 'Twas ever thus, and forever shall be."

A small crowd was gathering now. Expectant smiles. Gleaming eyes. Nervous laughter. They didn't know what was about to happen, but they knew it was bound to be somethin' else.

And that was, of course, when Lady Shelley floated in, so thin as to nearly be weightless.

"Oh, Lord Stanley," she tutted with self-righteous glee. "Making excuses for monstrosity again, I see. Why don't you just admit you get off on the atrocity? God knows you're not the only sadist here."

The crowd *ooohed*. I rolled my eyes, raised my hand, raised the planet off its platter, left it floating in the space between us.

"I suppose you'd like to coddle it," I countered. "Fill it up with whimsical fairy-dust breezes so mild they wouldn't tussle a dandelion's tuft, and cuddly creatures no self-respecting god could be bothered with."

"Why?" she replied. "So you could slap 'em around and shit on their heads? No thanks. I'll keep my dreams at a safe distance, if you don't mind terribly. Or even if you do… no, wait. *Especially* if you do!"

Ripples of derisive laughter echoed through the chamber. It was no secret that I'd been exceptionally cruel to her, and more than once. You'd think, given the sheer span of infinity, that maybe they'd cut me a fucking break. But no. Always with the 'But he's so *meeeean*!'

"I don't know why I even bother to come here," I muttered, more than loud enough to be heard. "It's like building a factory, just to make pearls for swine."

"Oh, heaven forfend!" she exclaimed with mock alarum. "What would we do without your genius!"

"Just because I'm not slopping over with your sickly sentimentality!"

"Yeah, or any other recognizable human emotion but contempt!"

"Now, now!" exclaimed the Muffleys, in unison.

"Shut up!" Lady Shelley and I both yelled, but not in solidarity. We just weren't done with each other yet.

On the little Earth I had floating between us, a trillion tiny humans had already evolved, fought, and died. If you looked closely, you could see their eentsy aeroplanes, circling the globe for what they doubtless supposed were very good reasons. On the one hand, it was kind of adorable. On the other, it was like gnats circling a turd.

It was the absurdity that made me laugh, of course. The earnestness and the pointlessness. The urge to greatness, and the certainty of doom. All creation was ridiculous. And yet, here we were. Over and over and over again.

I did not expect to find tears in my eyes. Was surprised as I blinked them back. Did she put them there? To punish? For perspective? Or was that just me, blindsided by feelings I didn't ask for, any more than I had asked to exist in the first place? I didn't know. But she was as surprised as me, her own eyes widening as she caught me in mid-act. And fool that she was, a tear came to hers as well. An unexpected empathy that made us both softly smile.

"I'm sorry," she said.

"You should be!" I mock-scolded. "No fighting in the War Room!"

She grinned back. "No eating in the Food Room!"

"No pooping in the Poop Room!"

"No fucking in the Fuck Room!"

And with that, we laughed and laughed. As the tiny world exploded. A miniature man, riding a bomb all the way down.

And with a whoop as loud as a mushroom cloud, Lady Ripper got off again.

DR. STRANGELOVE-1964

Razrez

by Craig Spector

"What's it going to be then, eh?"

First there was the krovvy—little dots and splotches like redred rain, or a child's game of connect the dots, or the dripdripdrip of a painter's like brush. Then the splotches grew to wild smears and swooshes, as if painted by Bog Himself in some mad arcing masterpiece… then an oozing pool, shining almost black in the fading light, but no, more deepest crimson, wafting little wisps of steamy steam in the chill dusky air.

But no, wait. Turn the clock hands back, then forward, like on a soft, drippy clock painted by mad artistos of old.

That was me, Your Humble Narrator, of lo so many annos past, when I was a mere malchick as it were, and not the starry silvered chelloveck now gracing your glazzies. It was way back, some fifty years in like Father Time's endless trudge toward Bog's Heavenly Host bleating over some dank and vonny hole, that the story of my young life had been seized upon, first by some writer type who turned it into a book—not a biography or such like, but more a novel, and with a great many things invented, O my Brothers and Sisters—and then later by some grand and bolshy sinny director who made me (or rather, the idea of me) and my once-upon-a-time droogs into an international star to viddy on the silver screen, in all our grand strack and ultra-violent glory.

All of which is fine and well, but it placed not a pound nor yen nor euro nor dengy dirty dollar into my grubby little rookers. Pretty polly and cutter aplenty for scribes and bugatti sinny stars who could titillate the lewdies on their screens and in the gazettas, but none for the chellovecks upon which the raskazz all depends. I did happen once to meet the chelloveck who played me onscreen; he seemed a likeable enough malchick and even I was surprised at our resemblance, like we could have been long-lost bratties.

It's true enough the fates of my fictitious-like droogs—old Pete and Georgie and Dim—had long since fled my gulliver with the grand ticktock of time: last I'd heard, Pete was all grown up-like and still selling insurance or some such dreck; fat gloopy old Dim eventually graduated from brute millicent to Honest to Bog prestoopnik himself, courtesy of his tendency to crack his truncheon into the litzos of regular citizens, until he finally got caught on viddy. He spent a plenny stretch up in the old Staja, and I didn't hear of him after, or much care to. And Georgie, well, Georgie just kind of disappeared without a dook, though by play fair or foul I know not.

Much the same with my latter-day shaika—Len, Rick, and Bully. But even by that long-ago time I was getting too starry to privodeet the malchicks for like, crasting and cracking and dratsing and the cry of britva to stir the krovvy and all; truth be told, my heart and mozg just weren't in it. So I cut them loose with falsely fond farewells, too, and went on my oddy knocky.

I did still have my rabbit at the National Gramodisk Archives, Music division—like the wretched and cursed Ludivico machine, that much was also true. I worked there for many annos, even got my own little cantora deep in the guttiwuts of a vast building done in early Brutalist style, all poured concrete and steel, with narrow oknos that let in light but no view, but walls thick enough that no one minded if I turned the music up for a proper sloosh.

And so life went on, as life is wont to do. I rabbited each day, and came home each night, to my room in the old Municipal Flatblock 18A, between Kingsley Avenue and Wilsonsway. In time pee and em passed—starry age and natural causes, if you care—and I inherited the old flat 10-8. It wasn't much, but doma was doma and it was my dorogoy own, and the new governments had cleaned up the flatblocks, painting over the ratty murals and lurid slovos and making things all habitable and civilized and such, with potted plants and stainless steel and marbled floors and walls. I got rid of the chepooka and redecorated in the latest fashion, which was very spare and austere but with a nozh-thin viddy screen that took up half the wall, and itty speakers that could boom lovely Ludwig Van or Mozart all through the dacha as I slurped my morning chai and munched lomticks of toast and jam before ittying off to another day's like labors.

As for Yours Truly, the ravages of Father Time were not entirely unkind: the voloss on my plott silvered prematurely and I kept it cropped; as my glazzballs blurred I came to wear little wiry otchkies. I kept trim and to fighting weight, and forsook the passing fashions of the days for simple, severe black—like a priest, say, or a ninja. But still, I was all on my oddy knocky and alone like—no devotchka nor comely ptitsa to come my way with heart beating pitter pat to civilize me. And no itsy witsy Alex babes, neither, to raise up and pass on the like wisdom of my experience. It seemed fitting, somehow, given the sheer ghastliness of my wayward nadsat days, what with the tolchocks and nozh scraps and dirty twenty-to-ones and other villainy of my youth.

Some days I missed that, but not often, my Brothers and Sisters. In the mornings and evenings I would walk along the waterway where I once cut Dim, or watch the news of the day as if viddying a piece of cinema, in which I was no longer the star but like an extra, or a member of the audience, all snug in my plush stadium surrounding sound seat, viddying what flickered across the screen.

These days it was a killer—aye, a nasty piece of clockwork, leaving his victims all bunched and splattered on the cold hard ground, arms tucked to hold in their stinking and steaming guttiwutts, and a single glazzball slashed and spattered.

And, said my dad, you were like helpless in your blood and couldn't fight back. Those slovos from my papapa of old, from one of his dreamy dreams. Or my own dream that very same day, of Georgie giving his general's orders and old Dim smecking around toothless as he wielded the whip… or Dim, soaked with greasy water and splatted with his own redred krovvy, a canvas for my own steely britva to paint, that long-ago day.

As I munched my morning toast and jammiwam and watched the viddy of the killer's latest victim, fallen not too far from old Flatblock 18-A, down by the waterfront, a part of my oomny messel was that this was no mutilator nor grahzny butcher. This was an artist. I felt the malenky hairs on the back of my gulliver stand at attention with the interressovat.

Once upon a wayback raz I would have recoiled, courtesy of Ludovico and his wretched machine, but as the annos passed the razdraz feelings like receded, and the vred to my rassoodock and plott gave way to a kind of polezny radosty—yes, almost joy, my Brothers and Sisters—when I viddied such nastiness. The urge to snuff it faded, replaced with like, nostalgia, almost, of glory days gone. It felt real horrorshow, if honest.

And then there was the malchick.

A malenky lad of maybe ten, who sat on the steps leading down to the harbor stroll, watching, like—dark hair mussed in the breeze, dark glazzies searching the horizon. I would viddy him sometimes as I goolied home from my Gramodisk rabbit and I wondered, who is this child, who looked for all the world like a young Alex, to my inner rassoodock's glazzy? Not some gloopy nadsat, but serious, thoughtful even—scanning the far horizon as if waiting for a ship to come in, or contemplating jeezny. But when I called out one day, all pleasant-like, "Oi, what's your eemya?" he got up and skorried off.

Probably saw me as some starry veck trying to get my rookers into his neezhnies.

I looked down then and saw the stain, where the krovvy plesk had seeped into the concrete like some modern art masterpiece, faint traces of the chalky outline from the millicents rendering the last victim's body in blocky oozhassny pose, doing herky jerky dance moves on the cold ground. I felt a vague chill and ittied off. It was like standing on the dead.

And so it went, my Brothers and Sisters, for like a fortnight— sometimes I'd viddy the malchick, sometimes not. And sometimes he was watched over by some mysterious devotchka dressed all in black, dark hair and pale green glazzies, taking in the whole scene with an odd smile, like she possessed some bolshoy amusing secret. And then they would both skorry off, leaving me to wonder.

Then one nochi I was ittying doma after a hard day's rabbit at the Gramodisc—it was dark early, like Autumn dark and a flip chill bastard though wet—bloshy dollops of rain painting the streets and walkways with an iridescent sheen. I had stopped off for a chassa of chai at a mesto near my cantora, then decided to cut through a pedestrian underpass to shorten my journey. As I paused to light a cancer it occurred to me that this particular underpass bore a striking resemblance to one from my long-ago youth, where young Alex and his droogs delivered some grahzny merzky tolchocks to some spoogy old drunky going all blurp blurp in his guttiwuts and yowling out to his forefathers until my boot landed square in his keehskas, and another boot to the gulliver shut him up good and proper. All for one and four on one, as were our preference.

It was right in mid-messel that I caught a glimpse of movement in the corner of one glazzie and looked over to see a slight figure stepping into view at the end of the overpass, and backlit all dramatic like. It was the cheena that I'd seen before, down by the wharf. She was dressed in a hooded cloak of some type, like some glamorous sinny star. She looked at me and gave a sly smile.

"Well well well," I said, trying to cover my surprise. "What can I do for you this fine nochy?"

It was only then that I heard the splish-splash of small feet, rapid upon me. As I turned, I felt a dull thump of contact near my waist, knocking me ever so slightly off balance—but as I righted myself and reached back my hand came back wet and red, so red it looked black in the halogen arc lamps. And I felt the first sting of pain as I recognized the malchick, running to the cheena, then turning to regard me, a dripping wet nozh in hand.

"Malenky bastard!" I cried out. "You cut me!"

I took a halting step forward, but too late slooshied another slapslapslap of feet, and felt another strike on my other side— this one sharper and deeper than the last. It knocked me off balance as I whirled, lashing out blindly. My otchkies went flying and I swung and missed, as a third then came from yet another angle, a low blow slicing at the back of my leg and cutting the cables behind my right knee, and down down down I went, like a wounded beast in a nature program on the telly, locked in a bitva as old as Time. Then came another, and another—maybe four or five in all, but honestly my pain-sotted mozg lost count, my Brothers and Sisters, as each took their turn with nozh and britva and shlaga, then all together as one, chopping your Humble Narrator to bits. And not one of them older than ten.

The cheena watched, a grimly prideful mother of the pack. It occurred to me that throughout the savaging, nary a sound had been made by my molody attackers, apart from the little grunts of their breath. Somewhere in the fray my own walking stick—its own artfully concealed nozh within—had skittered out of grasp, coming to rest near the cheena's feet. She picked it up as I lurched toward her, but as I grasped it in my krovvy-smeared rookers there was a click and a flash, and the cheena sunk my own blade deep in my brooko. It went in and up and across, a bolshoy arc that unzipped me from crotch to ribcage. I collapsed on the spot and awaited the inevitable crasting and pillage.

But none came, my Brothers and Sisters. As I clutched my brooko to keep my steaming keeshkas from uncoiling in the nochy air, I saw the oozhassny shaika of malenky prestoopniks, viddying the strack with great interest. And I realized, this was not oobivat for deng nor treasure nor cutter in my pocket. This was murder just to watch a chelloveck die.

And then I was out in the rain again, soaking to the skin in the cold cold night. I ploshed through puddles and stumbled down steps, heading toward the waterfront, with nary a soul to witness the jeezny leak out of me. At some point I stumbled and my rookers reached out to break the fall, but of course that freed my guttiwuts to spill forth with a ghastly splat, and there I lay, gazing up into the dark and stormy sky.

It was then, bled out and too weak to govereet or even creech, that a snatch of song ran through my bezoomny rassoodock—something from that long-ago sinny starring a make-believe Alex and his make-believe droogs.

"I'm s-singin' in the rain... just singin' in the r-rain..." I coughed up some dark dark krovvy. *"What a glorious f-feeling... I'm h-happy again...."*

And just like that, my Brothers and Sisters, I was gone.

A CLOCKWORK ORANGE - 1971

Role Play

BY RICHARD CHRISTIAN MATHESON

[INSPIRED BY 'EYES WIDE SHUT', 1999]

Tracing fingers over her perfect face.
"…so beautiful."
She sighs, empty.
Things inside him seem to shift.
"What do you want?"
"Hurt me…"
He looks at her. Stare draining black. Suddenly, slaps her cheek, "… like that whore?"
Scared. "…Yes."
 "Tell me."
 "Slap me…. harder."
Palm striking hard.
"What do you call me?"
Ashamed. "… Daddy."
"…but Daddy wouldn't like you doing this would he?"

"…No."

He wraps strong fingers around her pale neck. The bedside camera zooms.

"You love that. Don't you?"

She tries to speak.

"I said you love that… *don't* you?"

A whimper; child noises.

"You always want more because you're a dirty girl." He chokes her harder. Smiles cruelly. "Aren't you, *slut?*"

"…Yes, Daddy."

She struggles as he handcuffs her with one hand. "…Poor baby can't breathe?"

She gets wetter, skin trembling.

"Your husband knows all about your filthy secrets, doesn't he? How you crave being a whore?"

She whines; lascivious trance. Gasps at the size as he enters her fast, bites his muscled neck, pierces skin. Something inside him reacts. A tic of mouth. She spreads her legs wider. Body a delirium; sheets sweat-soaked. Squeezes him harder, tongue crawling lips.

"You ashamed to have a stranger's big cock inside you, slut?"

He thrusts deeper, makes her cry out; mouth a crimson wound.

"You wanna cum don't you, slut?"

She tries to push him away; starved for more.

The tic on his face gets worse. "…Gonna count to ten, slut. When I get to one… you can cum! Not before."

She looks away, breathes faster.

He grabs her chin. "Understand?"

She nods, begins to sob. Arches back.

"…eight… seven…."

She writhes. Rakes his cheek; red fingernails. Clutches tighter, feels it seething closer.

"…six…"

Tears run.

"…five… four…."

She rocks, frantic.

He gets to *two* when she starts falling from the cliff; insides uncaging; a raptured flood. Shudders; spasms. Tries prying his fingers from throat. Eyes begging. He grips harder, bruising soft skin, crushing trachea. Watches terror slowly drown her, as she collapses onto the sheets. Stares lifelessly.

He moves to wall mirror. Expression blank. Sees rip on cheek. Small cut on neck. Gets dressed. Sends text. DONE. Sits in dim bedroom. Blinks wrongly. Sensors malfunction, strong fingers spasm. Doesn't notice brochure on table:

CYBER TABOO

A.I. Technology
Programmable Fantasies
<u>Discrete Delivery / Available by the hour</u>
Terms and Conditions: *User engages services at own risk and agrees to waive all legal action. Units fully sanitized and de-programmed after each use.*

***

Across the world, her husband stares at the torture recording she'd sent. Bedside camera, as always, a perfect angle. Plays it, over and over; her beauty and tyranny, in close-up. Deceit in loveless eyes. Stops it before it's over; seen enough. It's always the same. Going too far, her obscene gift.

He feels himself. Numbed by her descriptions, mind leashed by the sordid images; other men, women. Couples. Lewd weaves of flesh. Her vulgar appetites a disease. Details he hates but can't live without.

One day, someday, if he was good, she'd promised to grant him permission; allow release of hungers she jailed inside him;

to finally climax. When she was ready, on that day, she'd whisper a single word she'd chosen just for him, the key to a locked cell she alone could open. Dominating and infecting his psyche with vicious hope.

He sighs, tired of it all. Wanting out. Loathing the vain cul-de-sac of her. Unable to flee. Needing to see the rest of the recording... all of it.

He presses PLAY.

Watches in horror as she gradually panics, choked harder, pleading. Clawing air, eyes stricken. Falling limply onto sheets. Strangled face; marble. He instantly sees the man is not real. A hired monstrosity. Imbecile malfunction. Just her style. Seeking thrills in the grotesque.

He watches the recording, again and again and again... wanting to throw up. Staring at her dead body. A woman he no longer knows. Touches himself more. Feels nothing; her mistress curse; despised addiction. He tries harder, hours passing, running countless words through his mind that don't work. Trying to think of more; the exact one. Frantically searching dictionary. Sensations trapped inside him like POWs. Desperate hand moving faster, as he weeps and bleeds.

Slowly smiles. It was so good.

EYES WIDE SHUT - 1999

About the Authors

ALESSANDRO MANZETTI (Rome, Italy) is a three-time Bram Stoker Award-winning writer, editor, scriptwriter and essayist of horror fiction and dark poetry. His work has been published extensively (more than 40 books) in Italian and English, including novels, short and long fiction, poetry, essays, graphic novels and collections.

English publications include his novels *Shanti - The Sadist Heaven* (2019) and *Naraka - The Ultimate Human Breeding* (2018), the novella *The Keeper of Chernobyl* (2019), the collections *The Radioactive Bride* (2020 and 2022) and *The Garden of Delight* (2017) the poetry collections *Dancing with Maria's Ghost* (2021), *Whitechapel Rhapsody* (2020), *The Place of Broken Things* (2019, with Linda D. Addison), *War* (2018, with Marge Simon), *No Mercy* (2017), *Sacrificial Nights* (2016, with Bruce Boston) *Eden Underground* (2015), *Venus Intervention* (2014, with Corrine de Winter), the graphic novels *Kraken Inferno* (2022), *The Inhabitant of the Lake* (2021), *Calcutta Horror* (2019), *Her Life Matters* (2020), and the essay/guide *150 Exquisite Horror Books* (2021).

His stories and poems have appeared in Italian, USA, UK, Australian, Canadian, Russian and Polish magazines. Website: WWW.BATTIAGO.COM

ALESSANDRO MANZETTI

About the Authors

Karen Runge is the author of *Seven Sins: Stories* (Concord Free Press), *Seeing Double* (Grey Matter Press), and *Doll Crimes* (Crystal Lake Publishing), which was later produced for Audible. Her standalone short stories are scattered across various magazines and anthologies.

Born in France to a travelling family, she later lived in the UK and in China before settling back in her native South Africa. A nature lover who prefers country life, she can often be found in the mountains near her home, climbing the cliffs or camping with her rescue dog. She is currently working on her third novel.

Website: HTTPS://KARENRUNGE.WORDPRESS.COM/

KAREN RUNGE

RICHARD CHRISTIAN MATHESON is an American writer and screenwriter, and is the son of Richard Matheson (author of the well known novel *I Am Legend*). He is the author of over 100 short stories of psychological horror and magic realism, published in more than 150 major anthologies and in his acclaimed short story collections, *Scars and Other Distinguishing Marks*, *Dystopia*, and *Zoopraxis*. His other works include the novel *Created by* and the novella *The Ritual of Illusion*. He edited the commemorative book *Stephen King's Battleground*, and adapted a short story for an iconic episode of the TNT series Nightmares and Dreamscapes, winning two Emmys. Among his works as a writer and/or co-writer: *Three O'Clock High*, *Full Eclipse*, *It Takes Two*, *Loose Cannons Shifter*, *Midvale*, *The Nature of Evil* (co-written with his father Richard Matheson), *Paradise*, *It Waits*, *Happy Face Killer*, *Voices of Midway*, "Red Sleep", "Hooky", Dean Koontz's Soul Survivor miniseries, three episodes of Masters of Horror, Stephen King's Big Driver and Nightmare Cinema. He wrote screenplays for Amazing Stories, for the miniseries Nightmares & Dreamscapes and adapted for miniseries HG Well's *The Time Machine*, Roger Zelazny's *The Chronicles of Amber*, and Whitley Strieber's *Majestic*.

JOHN SKIPP is an American writer, screenwriter and movie director, and is one of the founders of the Splatterpunk movement. He made his debut in collaboration with Craig Spector, with the novel *The Light at the End*. Over the following years he and Craig Spector wrote five other novels: *The Clean Up* (1987), *The Scream* (1988), *Dead Lines* (1989), *The Bridge* (1991) and *Animals* (1992). In 1985 he and Spector wrote the novelization of the film *Fright Night*, and in 1989 they edited the anthology *Book of the Dead*, dedicated to George Romero, and wrote the screenplay *A Nightmare on Elm Street 5: The Dream Child*—the fifth instalment of the famous movie series. After artistically separating from Craig Spector, he continued his career as a writer (and movie director) by publishing various works, including the novels *The Long Last Call*, *The Art of Horrible People* (2015), the collection of short stories, essays and screenplays *Don't Push the Button* (2021) and, co-written with Cody Goodfellow, *Jake's Wake* (2008), *The Day Before* (2009), *Spore* (2010) and *The Last Goddamn Hollywood Movie* (2013).

CRAIG SPECTOR is an American writer and screenwriter, and is one of the founders of the Splatterpunk movement. He made his debut in collaboration with John Skipp, with the novel *The Light at the End*. In the years that followed, the duo wrote five other novels: *The Clean Up* (1987), *The Scream* (1988), *Dead Lines* (1989), *The Bridge* (1991) and *Animals* (1992). In 1985, he and Skipp wrote the novelization of the movie *Fright Night*, and in 1989 they edited the anthology *Book of the Dead*, dedicated to George Romero, and scripted *A Nightmare on Elm Street 5: The Dream Child*—the fifth instalment of the famous movies series. After artistically separating from John Skipp, he continued his career as a writer by publishing various works, including the novels *To Bury the Dead* (2000), *A Question of Will* (2010), *Turnaround* (2013), *Underground* (2017). He also edited the short story anthology, *Freedom of Scretch*.

DAVID J. SCHOW (Marburg, 1955) is an award-winning American author and screenwriter living in Los Angeles. The last of his nine novels is a whimsical, hardboiled work titled *The Big Crush* (2019), while his most recent short story collections are *DJStories* (2018) and *Monster Movies* (2020). He has written many screenplays for film (*The Crow, Leatherface: Texas Chainsaw Massacre III, The Hills Run Red*) and television (Masters of Horror, Mob City). In addition to being one of Fangoria magazine's most popular columnists, he has also written non-fiction works, including *Outer Limits at 50* (2014) and *The Outer Limits Companion* (1998). As editor, he co-edited various titles with Robert Bloch (*The Lost Bloch*, three volumes, 1999-2002) and John Farris (*Elvisland*, 2004), as well as the legendary horror anthology *Silver Scream* (1988). He is featured as an expert or documentary filmmaker on various DVDs, including *Creature from the Black Lagoon* and *Psycho* to *I, Robot* and *King Cohen: The Wild World of Filmmaker Larry Cohen*. Thanks to his pioneering voice in the horror genre, the term "splatterpunk" entered the Oxford English Dictionary in 2002.

KUBRICK Rhapsody

BLACK MOUNTAIN
by Simon Bestwick
Novel – Paperback and eBook Edition
November 2021

APACHE WITCH
by Joe R. Lansdale
Poetry Collection – Hardcover Edition
September 2021

THE FEVERISH STARS
by John Shirley
Collection – Paperback and eBook Edition
March 2021

HER LIFE MATTERS
by Alessandro Manzetti and Stefano Cardoselli
Graphic Novel – Paperback Edition
December 2020

UMBRIA
by Santiago Eximeno
Collection – Paperback and eBook Edition
December 2020

LOST TRIBE
by Gene O'Neill
Novel – Paperback and eBook Edition
October 2020

SHILOH
by Philip Fracassi
Novella – Paperback and eBook Edition
October 2020

COYOTE RAGE
by Owl Goingback
Novel – Paperback and eBook Edition
February 2019

APARTMENT SEVEN
by Greg F. Gifune
Novella – Paperback and eBook Edition
Juanuary 2019

FEARFUL SYMMETRIES
by Thomas F. Monteleone
Collection – Paperback and eBook Edition
January 2019

DARK MARY
by Paolo Di Orazio
Novel – Paperback and eBook Edition
December 2018

TRIBAL SCREAMS
by Owl Goingback
Collection – Paperback and eBook Edition
October 2018

MONSTERS OF ANY KIND
Edited by Alessandro Manzetti & Daniele Bonfanti
Anthology – Paperback and eBook Edition
September 2018

ARTIFACTS
by Bruce Boston
Poetry Collection– Paperback and eBook Edition
July 2018

KNOWING WHEN TO DIE
by Mort Castle
Collection– Paperback and eBook Edition
June 2018

NARAKA
by Alessandro Manzetti
Novel– Paperback and eBook Edition
May 2018

A WINTER SLEEP
by Greg F. Gifune
Novel– Paperback and eBook Edition
April 2018

SPREE AND OTHER STORIES
by Lucy Taylor
Collection – Paperback and eBook Edition
February 2018

THE LIVING AND THE DEAD
by Greg F. Gifune
Novel – Paperback and eBook Edition
December 2017

TALKING IN THE DARK
by Dennis Etchison
Collection – eBook Edition
December 2017

THE BEAUTY OF DEATH 2 – DEATH BY WATER
edited by Alessandro Manzetti & Jodi Renee Lester
Anthology – Paperback and eBook Edition
November 2017

DREAMS THE RAGMAN
by Greg F. Gifune
Novella – Paperback and eBook Edition
November 2017

CHILDREN OF NO ONE
by Nicole Cushing
Novella – Paperback and eBook Edition
October 2017

THE RAIN DANCERS
by Greg F. Gifune
Novella – Paperback and eBook Edition
September 2017

THE WISH MECHANICS
by Daniel Braum
Collection – Paperback and eBook Edition
July 2017

THE ONE THAT COMES BEFORE
by Livia Llewellyn
Novella – Paperback and eBook Edition
May 2017

SELECTED STORIES
by Nate Southard
Collection – Paperback and eBook Edition
March 2017

THE CARP-FACED BOY AND OTHER TALES
by Thersa Matsuura
Collection – Paperback and eBook Edition
February 2017

DOCTOR BRITE
by Poppy Z. Brite
Collection – eBook Edition
December 2016

ALL AMERICAN HORROR OF THE 21ST CENTURY: THE FIRST DECADE
edited by Mort Castle
Anthology – Paperback and eBook Edition
November 2016

BENEATH THE NIGHT
by Greg Gifune
Novel – Paperback and eBook Edition
October 2016

WHAT WE FOUND IN THE WOODS
by Shane McKenzie
Collection – eBook Edition
September 2016

THE HORROR SHOW
by Poppy Z. Brite
Collection – eBook Edition
August 2016

THE BEAUTY OF DEATH VOL. 1
Edited by Alessandro Manzetti
Anthology – eBook Edition
July 2016

SELECTED STORIES
by Edward Lee
Collection – eBook Edition
July 2016

USED STORIES
by Poppy Z. Brite
Collection – eBook Edition
June 2016

THE USHERS
by Edward Lee
Collection – eBook Edition
May 2016

THE CRYSTAL EMPIRE
by Poppy Z. Brite
Novella – eBook Edition
April 2016

SONGS FOR THE LOST
by Alexander Zelenyj
Collection – eBook Edition
April 2016

SELECTED STORIES
by Poppy Z. Brite
Collection – eBook Edition
February 2016

THE HITCHHIKING EFFECT
by Gene O'Neill
Collection – eBook Edition
February 2016

9 791280 713575